# GET THE HELL OUT OF HERE

SHAWN M PENNINGTON

# GET THE HELL OUT OF HERE

*A Challenge to the Eternal Conscious Torment of Christian Dogma*

# PALMETTO
#### PUBLISHING
Charleston, SC
www.PalmettoPublishing.com

© 2024 Shawn M Pennington
All rights reserved.
No portion of this book may be reproduced,
stored in a retrieval system, or transmitted in
any form by any means—electronic, mechanical,
photocopy, recording, or other—except for
brief quotations in printed reviews,
without prior permission of the author.

All quotations from Scripture are taken
from the King James Version (KJV)
of the Bible unless otherwise noted.

Paperback ISBN: 9798822958364
eBook ISBN: 9798822958371

# CONTENTS

Hell at My Heels ............................................................. 1

Where the Hell? Hell in the Old Testament ................. 15

What the Gehenna? ..................................................... 25

Hell and the Parables ................................................... 35

The Rich Man and Lazarus .......................................... 63

A Hell of an Omission From the Apostle Paul ............. 71

All Hell Breaks Loose:
The Apocalypses of Daniel and Revelation .................. 83

Conclusion .................................................................. 95

Afterword .................................................................... 99

# HELL AT MY HEELS

When I was four years old, I stood in a cemetery with my mother. She lamented what a shame it was that Aunt Rose, the dearly departed, was headed to hell.

Thinking Mom must surely be mistaken, I reminded her that Rose was going to heaven, as she went to church every Sunday.

Mom replied, and I remember her words as clearly as if they were just spoken yesterday, "You can go to church every day of the week and still go to hell."

I did not know the meaning of the word *flabbergasted* at the time, but that is exactly the feeling that overcame me.

If sweet Aunt Rose—who, unlike me, actually enjoyed going to church—was headed to the Lake of Fire, what hope had I?

Thus began my relationship with hell, a mental battle that would plague me for more than the next fifty years.

For five full decades, hell has never been more than a few moments away from my thoughts.

I was raised as a Pentecostal, deep in the Appalachian Mountains. Church was central to our life, and hell was a regular topic, both inside and outside the sanctuary. I know of no denomination that preaches hell with quite the fervor and conviction of the Pentecostals. Even among Pentecostals, none preach it hotter or more frequently than the backwoods mountain variety of which I was a part.

When I was a child, a little white lie was met with not just a swat to the backside but also the admonition that all liars will have their part in hellfire. We were indoctrinated that taking part in worldly pleasures, such as a visit to the movie theater, might very well lead to one's eternal destruction. Daring to haphazardly miss church—which was held every Saturday night, Sunday morning, and Sunday evening, to cut down on the idle time available to us for sinning on the weekends, could certainly put one in danger of the fiery flames.

When I was seven years old, my father, who did not attend church, died. Being well versed in the fate of sinners, I had little hope for him having escaped the flames. During the following years, when I'd play with friends and begin to have a good time, the thought would so often occur to me: "How can I be having fun while my daddy is burning in hell?" And I'd sink back into the hell-inspired melancholy that I came to know so well.

Throughout childhood, I had heard enough about the suffering that awaited the wicked, which seemed to include most everyone, that I wanted no part of that dreadful place.

I had regular nightmares of running for my life while the earth around me was giving way and crumbling into the flames below. As I would, inevitably, begin to tumble into the fire, I would mercifully awaken and begin to pray to God to spare me such a horrific demise in real life.

Believing that fire and brimstone were about to begin raining down on me just any day, on December 31, 1978, as a ten-year-old child at an all-night New Year's Watch Service, I made my way to the altar, where I repented of my sins, dedicated my life to the Lord, was baptized, and received the gift of his Holy Spirit.

If I'm being honest, though, while bowing there at that altar, my thoughts were not primarily on how much I loved the Lord and how much I wanted to live my life for him. Instead, my plea was "Please don't send me to hell! Please don't send me to hell!"

I left that service so very relieved to finally be free from the threat of eternal torment!

My relief, though, was short-lived, as I was informed, soon thereafter, that we—unlike the Baptists, whose doctrine of "once saved, always saved" I came to envy—were more of the "once saved, good luck staying that way" belief.

As most things that interested me seemed to be sinful, and with the admonition that no sin can enter into heaven, I lived with the constant tension that even the smallest unrepented infraction could put me right back on that wide Path That Leadeth to Destruction!

With hell always biting at my heels, I repented, repeatedly, all throughout the day, each and every day, for sins known or unknown, lest I fall short of the requirements to someday make heaven my home and suffer in unspeakable torment forever.

Even into adulthood, I continued waging the never-ending mental battle of fighting off the doom of an impending hell. I have lived for decades with almost no moments of true peace of mind, and hell has always been at the center of my turmoil.

I have spent most of my life regretting that I had ever been born, the consequence of which was that I must now face the possibility of an eternity burning in the Lake of Fire. My near-constant dread overshadowed and diminished most any happiness in my life.

I say all of that to say this: there are probably very few people who have a more intimate relationship with the idea of eternal conscious torment in hell's fire than do I.

It has been, for many years, a part of the very fabric of my being, and I have little doubt that few have held as tightly as have I to the belief in the hell that is taught in Christian dogma.

While I did know that there were other religions and a multitude of sinners that held different views of hell than my own, the very concept that there actually existed *Christians* who did not hold to the idea of eternal torment in the afterlife never even entered my mind.

So, when I heard a pastor online state that hell was a place of total destruction and not a place of eternal conscious torment, I don't know whether I was more appalled at the perceived heresy of such a statement or more hopeful at even the possibility that it might be true.

Certainly, an eternal death sentence is nothing to be made light of, but compared to burning in agony forever and ever, it seemed like a walk in the park.

With no small amount of apprehension that perhaps I was sinning by even entertaining the idea that many whom I cared about—and possibly even myself—would not suffer for all eternity, I began to research the topic from another angle.

I read several books, written by theologians who have dedicated their lives to the study of Scripture, which endorsed the belief that what awaits the portion of humankind who will not enter onto Streets of Gold is a total separation, through eternal death, rather than burning in agony for all time.

Having the Bible's warning against false prophets, though, I was not about to abandon more than fifty years of hell-at-the-door theology to a few authors whose goal may have been little more than to deceive the very elect.

Doubtful, yet hopeful, that there was a measure of truth to what they taught, with a reverent and fearful heart, I approached God with the question of whether or not I had been wrong for so many years. Because I very much wanted that to be the case, but being careful not to just accept it for that very reason alone, I sought God's guidance on hell and eternity,

As is my habit, I got out of bed each morning at 4:00 a.m. for dedicated prayer time. In those predawn hours, I asked God to let me know His truth and to protect me from deceit. As much as I wanted a hell of eternal conscious torment to not be the reality, I wasn't going to abandon, without a fight that I didn't even want to wage, a lifetime's worth of hard-preached doctrine for some new-age, feel-good message.

One particular statement from my readings really struck at my heart, though:

*Infernalist Christians make up the only religion in which the members hold themselves to be morally superior to their God.*

While such a claim was shocking to even consider, there is truth to it.

Certainly, if I were forced to stand in judgment of my fellow man, I would never sentence anyone, regardless of their offense, to an *eternity* of unspeakable pain and continual suffering in which, after a trillion years of anguish, it would be as if they were only beginning their torment.

Yet how dare I, in my fallen state, consider myself to be more just, more compassionate, more loving than my God?

I quickly reasoned, *He's God. He can do as he sees fit. His ways are above my ways.*

All of that is definitely true, but I realized that my response was also just a way of me letting God off the hook for my perception that if He would assign such eternal torture, He was actually less just, less compassionate, and less loving than I.

That only holds true, though, *if* I adhere to the idea that He will actually issue such an eternal sentence of pain and anguish to those who missed the mark of His high calling.

Truly, His ways are above my ways, and in a much better capacity. He is, without any doubt, far more just, far more compassionate, and far more loving than I. Still, it was difficult to reconcile that my attributes were not above His if my concept of hell was true.

Whether I could make sense of it or not, with eternity at stake, I could not allow myself to surrender to human reasoning. I had to hold firmly to the Word of God, rather than yielding to my personal feelings.

With that reality in mind, I began to search the Scriptures, praying continually for understanding. I sought God as earnestly as I ever have, as I dared to consider the answer to whether or not hell was the place of eternal conscious torment that I believed it to be or, in truth, something much less horrible.

After much searching, praying, and fasting, I have come to believe that hell is a place of absolute destruction for the wicked. That, I have found, is exactly and completely what Scripture actually teaches and what I hope to demonstrate in the next few chapters. In reality, hell is not the place of continual torment that has been proclaimed from generation to generation, the result of errant Christian dogma.

I arrived at that conclusion solely by relying on Scripture, *as it is written*, rather than by how I had been conditioned to understand and interpret it.

During my search for the answer, rather than leaning on established church teachings, I allowed Scripture to clarify Scripture, a basic rule of hermeneutics.

I diligently sought God to open my understanding, and He has given me a clarity that has cleared the fog of church dogma that has stood, virtually unchallenged, for centuries.

So convinced am I in this truth that I now consider it to be bearing false witness against God to accuse him of sentencing people to an eternity of unimaginable suffering, to be impugning His very nature by charging Him with such.

I repent that I ever believed Him to be so unjust.

I understand that the reader who has not delved into the study as deeply might find my assertions to cross into heresy.

To that, I can only respond that I can't imagine anyone less likely than I to challenge the very concept of hell. Once I saw the truth of what hell actually is, though, I couldn't help but share it.

If I may be so presumptuous, perhaps it took someone so wholly invested in the teaching and belief of eternal torment as I to be able to spread, with such enthusiasm, the antithesis of that message.

I have been warned that some might respond to my claims in a hostile manner.

Perhaps I am naive, but just as when I was a young boy, I find myself flabbergasted that anyone would become angry about the possibility of hell not being a place of never-ending torment. Wouldn't such, if it were true, be welcomed with the same joy, relief, and gratitude that have flooded over me?

Certainly, I do understand becoming angry if someone perverts Scripture to fit into their own agenda. I will not do so. If I adhere to what Scripture actually says to support my view, I can only hope that any reader will, indeed, welcome the news.

I dare to think that even the most devout infernalist (one who believes in the eternal, fiery torment of hell) would be thrilled to learn that unsaved loved ones, and even most of the masses of people they pass daily on the street, are not bound for unspeakable doom.

Again, we can't base our judgment on feelings, but rather on only what the Word of God says. To that Word, rather than to the church dogma that has been the official stance of Christianity since not so very long *after* the teaching of the early apostles, I remain committed.

I've heard it said and tend to agree that very often the Bible is not actually our authority on how we live and believe. Our doctrine and our traditions are our authority, and we just read the Bible in such a way as to support what we already hold true.

By allowing the Bible to be my actual authority on hell, for the first time in my life, I have true peace of mind.

I now know how the Psalmist felt when he proclaimed, "I sought the Lord, and He answered me and delivered me from all my fears!" (Ps. 34:4).

I have fallen deeper in love with the Lord than ever before, and I now have the assurance that I follow him because of that love and because he is so very worthy, and not because I was so desperately holding on to a hopeful "Get Out of Hell Free" card.

I pray that others who have battled the mental anguish of a possible eternity in hell for themselves or their loved ones may find solace as well.

In the next few chapters, I will discuss how I came to this conclusion. Please do not write me off as a seed that has become choked by the thorns until, at least, you have reached the end. I pray that will not be your final conclusion.

Before we go on, though, please indulge me by reading the three statements contained in the following triangles and the jumbled quote that follows.

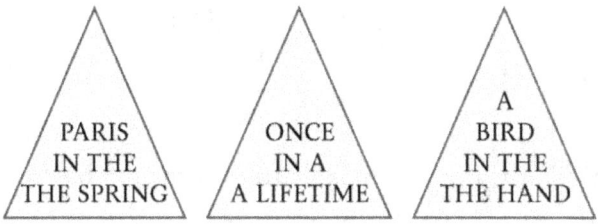

If you, like most people, read "Paris In The Spring," "Once In A Lifetime," and "A Bird In The Hand" in the triangles, I'd ask you to go back and read them once more.

Did you catch the differences that time?

The statements actually read, "Paris In The The Spring," "Once In A A Lifetime," and "Bird In The The Hand."

If you read them the former way, it's simply because the brain, when its familiar with a subject, is conditioned to read what it thinks something says without any real thought to what it *actually* says.

> 7H15 M3554G3
> 53RV35 7O PR0V3
> H0W 0UR M1ND5 C4N
> D0 4M4Z1NG 7H1NG5!
> 1MPR3551V3 7H1NG5!
> 1N 7H3 B3G1NN1NG
> 17 WA5 H4RD BU7
> NOW, ON 7H15 LIN3
> Y0UR M1ND 1S
> R34D1NG 17
> 4U70M471C4LLY
> W17H 0U7 3V3N
> 7H1NK1NG 4B0U7 17,

Similarly, if you were able to read the jumbled message above, it's because the brain is conditioned to add what it believes is missing, to use learned logic to make sense of things, and to see things as one imagines them to be rather than how they actually are.

So it is with Scripture, sometimes. Even when no mention of eternal suffering is a part of a passage concerning hell, the mind, conditioned by nearly two thousand years of Christian dogma, will insert such views into the verses as if they are actually written there. The mind will fully interpret what it thinks a verse is saying even if, in reality, it is not at all what the Scripture actually says.

As we continue, I will use only Scripture, in context and as it is written, to justify my position. I will not take anything away from the passages and ask only that you not add anything extra to them.

Except in a very few cases, which will be noted, I will use only the King James Version (KJV) of the Bible. Goodness knows, I'm already asking much of you. I dare not stray from the KJV as well!

One final note: To do a detailed study, it is helpful, if not imperative, to know what the verses actually said in their original Hebrew (for the Old Testament) or Koine Greek (for the New Testament).

I, as previously disclosed, am an Appalachian hillbilly and am barely able to speak acceptable English, much less Hebrew or Greek.

When referring to such languages, I will be using the online translator tool from www.biblehub.com. I encourage you to verify each time I reference the original language of the Scripture by using this or any other translator tool as you see fit.

# WHERE THE HELL?
# HELL IN THE OLD TESTAMENT

I'm familiar with the adage "If it's true, it isn't new, and if it's new, it isn't true."

Certainly, we must be cautious and meet with much skepticism whenever a teaching arises that goes against tradition.

Paul told the church at Thessalonica, "So then, brothers, stand firm and hold to the traditions that you were taught by us…" (2 Thess. 2:15) but we are also cautioned, "So for the sake of your tradition you have made void the word of God" (Matt. 15:6).

Letting go of a tradition that has been a part of the very bedrock of one's faith for as long as one can recall is no small thing.

Paul warned, "But even if we or an angel from heaven should preach a gospel other than the one we preached to you, let him be eternally condemned!" (Gal. 1:8).

That is no small thing for you, and even more so for me, to consider!

I hope I will show, in the pages ahead, that neither Paul nor Jesus nor any of the original apostles actually taught a message that included a place of eternal torment for humankind. As such, I'm bringing no new gospel, but rather adhering to the *original* gospel message.

As for the gospel message, I hold firmly to the Path of Salvation being through Jesus, my Savior, who was born of a virgin, lived a sinless life, died as my perfect sacrifice to redeem me through his shed blood, and rose again, victorious over death, hell, and the grave.

What I am sharing in these chapters, though, has nothing to do with the salvation message. I am more addressing the damnation message and what that damnation actually means.

While my interpretation is, no doubt, different from what you, your parents, or your grandparents (going back until about AD 55) heard, it truly isn't new.

Rather, I hearken back to something quite old: the teachings, or lack thereof, of hell found in the Hebrew Bible (which contains the same books as our Old Testament), the teachings of the Early Church in the New Testaments, and, yes, even the teachings of Jesus.

When I prayed, I asked, "Lord, let me know what you actually taught, for you are the authority, and whatever your words actually say is the truth that I want to follow."

We will cover the parables taught by Jesus concerning hell in just a couple of chapters. That may sound like a long time to wait to prove me wrong, and you may want to jump ahead, but there are only a few pages to go. We'll get there shortly You can do it! I know you can!

For now, though, let's start back at the very beginning, with the Old Testament.

The teachings we find in that volume cover approximately fifteen hundred years, spanning from around 2000 BC to about 400 BC.

The Old Testament era was a time when God spoke much more clearly to his people than he does today. We certainly still hear from God, but, at least for me, it isn't quite the same as the actual conversations, shared between the patriarchs of the Old Testament and Yahweh.

God spoke to Moses through the burning bush. By his own hand, he wrote the Ten Commandments that Moses carried to the Israelites. He spoke with Abraham about sacrificing Isaac and bargained with him to save Lot and his family from Sodom. He gave visions to the prophets and gave Joseph the ability to interpret dreams, and that is only scratching the surface.

God made His will known to His people and laid things out very clearly for them. At every turn He guided them. When they were wrong, He warned them. When they needed laws to function as the society that God wished them to be, He spoke those regulations to Moses.

Chapter after chapter in the Old Testament is, in fact, taken up with the Law of Moses. It was these laws by which the Children of God would live and by which they would be punished if they did not adhere to those regulations.

Moses had some very detailed conversations with God, it appears. He was given 613 laws to share with the Israelites, and each law came with its own specific penalty if transgressed.

God was very clear about what would happen to those who disobeyed the law.

For redemption, some infractions required a lamb to be sacrificed upon the altar. Some required a male goat, others required the sacrifice of a female goat, and still others could only be rectified with the sacrificial blood of a young bull.

People, too, paid with their own blood.

If a woman committed adultery, she was to be stoned to death. If a man indulged in bestiality, both he and the unfortunate animal were to be executed. If one got into a drunken brawl in the wine tent, pulled out their sword, and cut off their opponent's hand, their own hand was to be hacked off to pay for their crime. If someone stole, they had to return what they had taken plus an additional 20 percent of the value on top of that. If an unmarried woman had sexual relations with an unmarried man, she got off pretty easily, suffering nothing more than a prohibition from ever marrying a priest. If that single lady indulging in fornication happened to be a priest's daughter, however, she was to be burned at the stake for dishonoring her father.

The list of punishments goes on and on and reveals the very detailed communication, which God and Moses entered into together, about the consequences of sin.

In all those discussions concerning penalties, though, not one time did God ever mention anything to Moses about a place of never-ending torment into which transgressors would be cast to suffer eternally after their death.

Throughout the fifteen-hundred-year span of the Hebrew Bible (Old Testament), not one time was there ever mentioned a realm of eternal torment for the dead.

It's not as if the idea of unpleasant conditions in the afterlife was unknown at the time. The Israelites' neighbors throughout Mesopotamia—the Sumerians, the Babylonians, the Assyrians, to name just a few—all held to a belief of an afterlife that could include great suffering. The Jews, though, remained the only culture in the Levant to not only worship a single God but also to hold no concept of anything even remotely close to what we think of today as hell. The God of Israel simply did not punish his people in such a way and never communicated anything at all about such a place to His children.

Unfortunately, when we consult our Old Testament rather than the Hebrew Bible—which, again, has the same books but maintains the original wording used by the authors—we find that the translators of the King James Version of the Bible were a "hell-happy" bunch. They liberally sprinkled the term *hell* for this word or that word throughout both the Old and New Testaments, even when the actual words used by the authors were very distinct and had meanings far too varied to all be lumped, as the translators chose to do, under the single term "hell."

Don't choke when I say this, but those KJV translators, by doing so, were misleading at best—deceitful at worst.

I suppose we can cut them a little slack, though. In their defense, they were well into the era of hell, as we know it, as the official church dogma.

Dante's *Inferno* also had already hit the street as a bestseller. It is upon this literary work, rather than the Bible, that most of our concepts of hell have been formed.

Those priests of the Church of England, who undertook the work of translation for King James, were not very far removed from the dark Middle Ages, when pious living and the constant threat of hell were a part of daily life.

During that period (and, dare I say, even today) the concepts of hell and the torture that awaits there were reinforced at every turn by the church, which held much political sway at the time. The horrors that awaited those who strayed from the righteous path, as presented by the church, were used to keep the masses of common folk in line. Indeed, hell was then taught about in ways that would make even a Pentecostal preacher shiver.

So, if something even hinted of hell, those interpreters were going to give hell full billing.

In the Hebrew Bible, though (which, again, comprises the same books as our Old Testament, just with the original language), there is absolutely no mention of hell anywhere. Absolutely nowhere at all.

What the Jews knew, as a place for the dead, was Sheol, the grave.

In the KJV of the Bible, the translators rendered a great many of the sixty-six mentions of Sheol as "hell." Not even in their translations, though, was there any indication of a place of eternal conscious torment. Indeed, there was no mention of any punishment at all beyond the death they had suffered—for anyone.

Sheol was simply the abode of the dead.

The Jews didn't believe that the soul existed separately from the body, so when the body died, the soul did as well.

The Psalmist lamented that, once in Sheol, they were utterly forgotten about, by even God.

Both the most righteous of the dead and the most wicked of the dead went to Sheol together. There was no separation for them in the hereafter, regardless of how they had lived their lives. They all ended up in the same place.

Surely, if the Israelites, God's chosen people, were in error in their belief of the afterlife and they needed to do something to avoid an eternity of burning in the Lake of Fire, God would have spoken a warning to Moses or one of the other patriarchs to pass on to the people.

God's silence on the subject is deafening.

Hell, as we know it, simply did not exist for the Hebrews.

Inasmuch as it did exist outside the writings of the Hebrew Bible / Old Testament, it was not something about which the children of God needed to concern themselves, for it was a place that had been created only for Satan and the fallen angels. That wretched place, Tartarus, just like the much more benevolent Sheol, is also referred to in the KJV, the single time that it is mentioned in the Bible, simply as hell.

Beyond the realm of the devil and his fallen angels, alluded to in Isaiah, there is absolutely no record of a place of eternal torment in the Hebrew Bible or in the Old Testament.

All those prophets foretelling the end of times, the destruction to come along with God's judgment, all those early fathers of the Jewish people who regularly communed with God, and there is not one word about the place we know as hell. Not even a hint of such a place.

Let that sink in.

# WHAT THE GEHENNA?

As I have researched and discussed this topic with others, I have repeatedly heard or read from those with an opposing view that "Jesus taught about hell more than anyone!"

But did he really teach about the place which we know as hell, or was it something very different that he actually taught his disciples? To properly analyze that question, we must first familiarize ourselves with Gehenna.

Why must we care about Gehenna? Simply because Jesus never once uttered the word "hell."

I can almost hear you shouting, "Yes, he most certainly did!!"

Take a moment. Wipe up your drink if you knocked it over when your hand slapped the table, and give that temporal vein, which is about to pop, a moment to subside.

In actuality, each and every time in Jesus's parables of Matthew and Mark, when Jesus taught about the fate of the wicked, the word he actually used was not *hell* but rather *Gehenna*.

Just as they had done with Sheol and Tartarus, it was the KJV translators, so entrenched in the church's dogma of hell and eager to portray images of a fiery afterlife, who substituted the term *hell* into the parables rather than using Jesus's actual word, "Gehenna."

So, what's up with Gehenna?

Known by various names—the Valley of Hinnom, Ge-hinnom, the Valley of Slaughter, the Valley of Wailing, and Topeth—Gehenna is a literal valley just outside the walls of Jerusalem.

From the time of the prophets Jeremiah and Isaiah, and carried over into the time of Jesus, few places were held as more contemptible than Gehenna.

During Old Testament times, Judah's kings, for generations, had sacrificed Jewish children in that valley to the false god Baal.

In his wrath, God declared that Judah would pay a great price for their sins: that they would be defeated in battle, and mass death (the wage of their sin) would befall them. The fallen Israelites would be discarded in Gehenna until there was no room for more bodies, and their carcasses would become food for the birds and wild animals (Jer. 7:30–34).

Scripture makes it clear that Gehenna was a place cursed by God, a place with an abominable legacy, a despicable place where no one wished to end up.

Many scholars have also declared that Gehenna served as Jerusalem's garbage dump, where the city's trash and animal carcasses were disposed of, and even bodies of criminals, enemy soldiers, or other degenerates who were not given proper burials were set ablaze.

In the Jewish culture, such an improper burial was the height of disgrace. Ecclesiastes 6:3–4 teaches that even if a man has one hundred children and lives a very long life, if he is given an improper burial, it would have been better for him to have been stillborn rather than ever entering into life.

There was no place more abominable to meet such a disgraceful fate than Gehenna.

Isaiah—later quoted by Jesus, who placed Isaiahs's prophecy in Gehenna—foretold that the enemies of God would meet their demise and that they would be consumed by fire and worms. The children of God would look upon the dead bodies (carcasses) with contempt: "And they shall go forth and look upon the carcasses of the men that have transgressed against me: for their worm shall not die, neither shall their fire be quenched and they shall be an abhorring unto all flesh" (Isa. 66:24).

Certainly, Isaiah's prophecy can be taken as an eschatological (relating to the End Times) reference, and Jesus certainly used it that way when he quoted it in Mark 9:48, but in his vision, Isaiah was actually seeing the end of the Assyrian Army destroyed under King Hezekiah. In Isaiah's literal prophecy, he saw the corpses being burned with fire and eaten by worms, but his usage of the fire being not quenched and the worms not dying is figurative rather than literal. The enemy was indeed burned and devoured, but the fire did come to an end once its work was complete, and the worms are not, in reality, still feasting today on the long-dead Assyrians.

While many will quote this verse as foreshadowing hell, do note that Isaiah used the word *carcasses*, which are dead bodies, not bodies preserved alive for the purpose of suffering. Isaiah neither saw nor prophesied that the enemies of God would remain alive to suffer torment. Rather, he saw and foretold of the disgraceful annihilation of the wicked.

As a side note, after the time of Jesus, some rabbis, influenced by pagan Greek beliefs of the afterlife, did teach that Gehenna was a place of spiritual purification for the wicked dead. In their version, they limited the punishment to between three and twelve months, depending on the severity of the offense. Additionally, the condemned were given the Sabbath day off from being disciplined, free to do as they wished—or at least as much as the dead could do while on a bout of R and R—but were required to return late Saturday evening (the Jews celebrate the Sabbath from sundown on Friday to sundown on Saturday) to resume their penal sentence. After their temporary exile in Gehenna, during which they were punished appropriately, they would join the righteous in the world to come.

While I include this anecdote since it does refer to Gehenna as a place of temporary punishment, I don't imagine many Christians will give it serious consideration, nor should they. Following teaching inspired by Greek mythology to form Christian religious beliefs is not something to which Christianity should ascribe. (If you agree with that statement, please hold that thought for later when I'll be asking you, once again, to agree with that sentiment.)

Rabbi Maimonides, one of the most influential Torah (Books of Moses) scholars of the Middle Ages, declared that the descriptions of Gehenna as a place of punishment in rabbinic literature were *inventions by the rabbis* to encourage respect for the Torah (aka scare followers into submission) and that the actual Jewish stance was that rather than being temporarily sentenced to Gehenna, the unrighteous would, in fact, simply be annihilated.

This official Jewish teaching of the total destruction of the wicked certainly aligns with the teachings of the Hebrew Bible (Old Testament) and the many examples of annihilation of the enemies of God set therein.

Depending on the context, then, Gehenna is a literal place of destruction and contempt to those who were familiar with it (which virtually all Jews during the time of Jesus would have been) or, as in Isaiah 66:24, a figurative place of judgment where the unrighteous will be punished by a dishonorable death (often with the burning of the bodies).

At no time in history, though, was Gehenna presented as or understood to be a place in which the wicked will suffer for eternity. Again, eternal conscious torment in the afterlife was simply not a belief taught by God to His people. The Jews, aside from those who were influenced by pagan Greek mythology, had no concept of such a place as what we call hell. The parables of Jesus, which, symbolically, taught being cast into Gehenna as punishment for the unrighteous, would never have been interpreted by the listeners of the time as meaning a place of eternal torment. They would have understood the fate of those cast into Gehenna to be disgraceful deaths.

If, for example, we heard a news report that someone had become lost in the wilds of Alaska and perished due to the cold, nobody would interpret that to mean that the one who perished was still alive, freezing for all eternity. Rather, they would interpret such a statement to mean that the one who perished, died. We have never been conditioned to think otherwise. So, it was with Jesus's disciples. When Jesus taught that anyone was cast into Gehenna (which those KJV translators insisted on calling "hell"), those hearing the message would have interpreted it to mean that they died a fiery death. That they perished. That they were annihilated. They had never been conditioned to think otherwise.

It was, therefore, annihilationism, not infernalism, that Jesus actually taught.

Isaiah, with his vision of unquenchable fire and the worm that does not die, certainly evokes images of our concept of hell. Allowing Scripture to clarify Scripture, though, the unquenchable fire of Gehenna simply meant that it would not be extinguished until its work was thoroughly complete. Such vivid phrasing is common throughout the Bible and is often not meant to be taken literally.

As examples, Matthew 3:12 and Luke 3:17 share the parable from John the Baptist in which he states that the chaff (the outer covering of wheat that is not suitable for consumption) will be burned with unquenchable fire.

A parable is an easily understood and relatable story that presents a simple everyday example for the listener that can be interpreted for spiritual teaching. Those to whom John spoke would have had an understanding that the unquenchable fire would burn hot and all-consuming until the chaff was destroyed, turned to ash, completely obliterated. At that point, the fire would not continue to burn but would extinguish itself once its work was completed. There would have been no concept or even a reason to suspect, by the crowd who heard the parable, that what John referred to as unquenchable fire would continue to burn forever once the chaff was destroyed.

Similarly, Jude 1:7 states, "Just as Sodom and Gomorrah and the surrounding cities, which likewise indulged in sexual immorality and pursued unnatural desire, serve as an example by undergoing a punishment of eternal fire."

As the fate of Sodom and Gomorrah is declared to be an example for us, let's indeed apply it for our understanding of what the Scripture says. Clearly, Jude states that Sodom and Gomorrah were punished by *eternal fire*. Even as Jude wrote that verse, though, the flames that consumed Sodom and Gomorrah had been extinguished for centuries.

Today, the sites of those two fallen cities are not still aflame. The eternal fire of our example was not meant literally to be eternal but meant that it would burn until its job was completed, until the cities and the occupants therein were totally destroyed.

In the figurative, rather than the literal, the fire of God's judgment is eternal, and the destruction of his wrath is the example that still burns.

Additionally, prophesying concerning the Land of Edom, Isaiah 34:9–10 (our same author of the unquenchable fire of Gehenna) declares, "Edom's streams will be turned into pitch, her dust into burning sulfur, her land will become blazing pitch! It will not be quenched night or day; its smoke will rise forever."

The Land of Edom is today occupied by Israel and Jordan, and it is not currently aflame. Isaiah's blazing pitch that would not be quenched was in actuality extinguished once its work of destruction was complete, and his prophetic smoke that would rise forever is, in truth, no longer billowing.

Clearly the Bible uses such evocative language as figurative rather than literal. So, it is with the unquenchable fire of Gehenna.

Rabbi Maimonides affirmed the ending of the wicked by utter destruction to be what the Hebrew Bible (upon which the teachings of Jesus were based) actually taught.

Indeed, there is much found in Scripture to support an ending that leads to the absolute destruction of the wicked, such as what took place in Gehenna. There is, though, absolutely no example anywhere in Scripture to indicate an eternal torment for humankind.

(Hold your horses. We'll discuss Lazarus and the Rich Man as well as the Book of Revelation in just a bit.)

# HELL AND THE PARABLES

The parables of Jesus, especially in the Book of Matthew, certainly mention a lot about hell. Again, though, that fact is courtesy of the priests from the Church of England who translated the Scripture for King James. They used the term "hell" willy-nilly to give visions of a fiery eternal fate for the unredeemed, despite the words actually used in the original Hebrew or Koine Greek indicating no such thing.

I realize that I am repeating key points. I do so unapologetically. Hell has been reiterated in churches week after week. A lifetime of having hell driven into one's mind may require more than a single mention of an opposing view to chip away at the errant church dogma that has become the accepted reality of virtually all saints.

Please bear with me as I try to drive the points home with all the conviction, but less of the sprayed spittle, of a worked-up, fire-and-brimstone preacher on a Sunday morning.

As noted in the last chapter, what Jesus actually said in the parable was not hell, but Gehenna.

As we just discussed, Gehenna is absolutely not a synonym of the hell that we know.

To the disciples, who were being taught these parables by Jesus, Gehenna would have conjured up images of a God-forsaken place where fire burned disgraced corpses to their complete annihilation as worms ate the flesh from the bone. The reality of Gehenna, as it was understood by the disciples, was that the enemies of God would die and burn to ash and that their memories (carcasses) would serve as a source of everlasting contempt (disgust, disdain) to the righteous (Isa. 66:24).

The reason Jesus used the image of Gehenna to illustrate what would happen on the Day of Judgment to the wicked rather than using the Aramaic word (the common language of Jews at the time) for a place of eternal suffering when he instructed his apostles was, again, because *no such word, no such place* existed in the Hebrew language.

The Jews' doctrine, upon which Christianity was founded, held no concept of a place of eternal torment following death. That point simply cannot be reiterated enough.

Jesus taught his disciples from the Hebrew Bible (Old Testament). Had he suddenly began teaching a doctrine of eternal conscious torment following death, his disciples would have questioned why he was abandoning their faith in favor of bringing in the mythologically based doctrine of the pagans.

The disciples would have very much understood that death (total destruction, complete annihilation) of the wicked, particularly through the fire of God's judgment, was a price commonly paid for bringing God's wrath. Such a fate for the wicked was a common event in the Scriptures of the Hebrew Bible.

Jesus used the term Gehenna, symbolically, to paint a prophetic picture of the abhorrent destruction (death), by the fire of God's retribution, that awaits the wicked at the Great White Throne Judgment.

Before we go into the parables, upon which we may very well disagree, let's at least agree on one point:

*The wage of sin is Death (Rom. 6:23).*

Jesus, on Calvary, gave his life as our perfect sacrifice to cover our transgressions with his blood. The wage of our sin (death) was paid in full by our Savior.

If, however, infernalists are correct, then the price of sin is not actually death. In the doctrine that teaches burning forever in hell as the consequence of sin, death is just a portal through which the wicked pass as they go on to pay the actual price of sin, an eternity of torment in the flames.

Consider this, though:

> *If infinite torment and suffering are the actual prices we must pay for sin, then the finite death of Jesus on Calvary was not sufficient to pay the wage.*

If infernalists are correct, then we still owe a balance for our transgressions because while Jesus paid the wage of death, he did not take on an eternity of suffering in hell on our behalf.

The good news, though, is that Scripture, rather than Infernalist Church dogma, is true. Death, not eternal torment, is indeed the required wage of sin, and Jesus paid that price in full: "For God so loved the world that He gave His only begotten son, that whosoever believeth in him should not perish but have everlasting life" (John 3:16).

The word "perish" means to suffer death, typically in a violent manner. In absolutely no context does perish mean the polar opposite of death. Being preserved alive, even in a state of torment, requires everlasting life, which is the very antithesis of perishing. Everasting Life is a promise to those who believe, not a curse to those who do not.

Those who do not accept the gift of salvation must pay the price of sin (death, perishing) on their own behalf.

If not alive at the Second Coming of Christ, we will all die the first death, that of our actual flesh.

It is, though, the second death that will destroy both body and soul in hell (or in Gehenna, as Jesus actually said in Matthew 10:28).

Just like *perish*, *destroy* does not, in any capacity, mean to be preserved alive, even for suffering. *Destroy*, used by Jesus to describe the fate of the unredeemed, also means just the opposite of Eternal Life.

The second death, a fulfilment of Romans 6:23, as we will discuss in the chapter on Revelation, is the ultimate and final price of sin for those whose names are not found in the Book of Life.

OK, let's finally get into those Parables.

I'm gonna dive right in and address the "big one," the Parable of the Sheep and the Goats, first. This parable, especially, is used to support the idea of an eternity spent suffering in hell. Per Matthew 25:31–46:

31 When the Son of Man comes in his glory and all the angels with him, he will sit on his glorious throne,

32 All the nations will be gathered before him, and he will separate the people one from another as a shepherd separates the sheep from the goats.

33 He will put the sheep on his right and the goats on his left.

34 The king will say to those on his right, "Come, you who are blessed by my Father, take your inheritance, the kingdom prepared for you since the creation of the world.

35 For I was hungry and you gave me something to eat, I was thirsty and you gave me something to drink, I was a stranger and you invited me in,

36 I needed clothes and you clothed me, I was sick and you looked after me, I was in prison and you came to visit me."

37 Then the righteous will answer him, "Lord, when did we see you hungry and feed you, or thirsty and give you something to drink?

38 When did we see you a stranger and invite you in, or needing clothes and clothe you?

39 When did we see you sick or in prison and go to visit you?"

40 The king will reply, "Truly I tell you, whatever you did for one of the least of these brothers and sisters of mine, you did for me."

41 Then he will say to those on his left, "Depart from me, you who are cursed, into the eternal fire prepared for the devil and his angels.

42 For I was hungry and you gave me nothing to eat, I was thirsty and you gave me nothing to drink,

43 I was a stranger and you did not invite me in, I needed clothes and you did not clothe me, I was sick and in prison and you did not look after me."

44 They also will answer, "Lord, when did we see you hungry or thirsty or a stranger or needing clothes or sick or in prison and did not help you?"

45 He will reply, "Truly I tell you, whatever you did not do for one of the least of these, you did not do for me."

46 They then will go away to eternal punishment but the righteous to eternal life.

In this parable, we find the Son of Man, on his throne, with his angels. Clearly, this is meant to illustrate events occurring at the Great White Throne Judgment.

The righteous and the unrighteous are separated, each to go either to their eternal reward or to their eternal punishment.

The eternal reward is—I'm sure we'll agree—eternal life in heaven.

But what of the eternal punishment?

Clearly, Jesus says the goats will be cast into the eternal fire that was prepared for the devil and his angels. I'm quite certain we're still in agreement.

Where we are, no doubt, going to start to differ is in this: Just what, exactly, is the eternal punishment, and what is the result of being cast into the eternal fire?

Nothing here, or anywhere else in Scripture, says that the unrighteous humans cast into the fire are going to be preserved alive and continue in torment for all eternity.

I understand that's how you read it. I read it that same way for decades. It absolutely is not what it says, though.

The disciples to whom Jesus taught this parable, again, had no concept of a place of continual suffering after death. They would not have considered, for even one moment, that those cast into the eternal fire meant for the devil and his angels would be miraculously transformed into immortal beings who would be tormented forever and ever. They would have understood the end result to be that those cast into the fire would perish, suffering death for all eternity.

It is the infernalist Christians who, based on traditions taught by errant Church dogma, extend immortality to the lost (even though the gift—or, in this case, the curse—of immortality is nowhere in Scripture extended to the unrighteous). It is the infernalist's preconceived notion, not Scripture, which has the lost preserved forever and ever in eternal conscious torment.

Even in the absence of any evidence that it will happen, the Christian reader fully "understands" eternal torment to be the case once thrown into the fire. Just as in our word puzzles in chapter 1, the mind accepts such a conclusion as being perfectly valid, even though it's nowhere to be found in the scripture.

Such a belief, though, would have been considered pagan mythology both by the disciples who heard that parable and by the Savior who taught it.

As much as I'd like to wait to jump ahead to Revelation, it needs to be addressed at this point to shore up the claim I have just made concerning death, not eternal conscious torment, being the eternal punishment.

So, let's skip ahead a moment from Matthew, the first book of the New Testament, to Revelation, the last book.

The following verses, just like the parable of the sheep and goats, takes place at the Great White Throne Judgment (Rev. 20:10 and 20:14–15):

10 And the devil that deceived them was cast into the lake of fire and brimstone, where the beast and the false prophet are, and shall be tormented day and night for ever and ever.

14 And death and hell were cast into the lake of fire. This is the second death.

15 And whosoever was not found written in the book of life was cast into the lake of fire.

I know, I know. This sure enough sounds exactly like it supports the hell you were expecting and in which you believe. It truly is not. Keep a mind opened by prayer for understanding, and consider the following:

Verse 10 states that it is *specifically* the devil, the beast and the false prophet, who will be tormented day and night forever and ever in this place that was created *specifically* for the devil and his angels.

The devil, we are all familiar with. I am no expert on End Time prophecy (nor on very much else, to be honest), so I am going to discuss the beast and the false prophet only sufficiently to make a point.

Revelation 13 describes the beast as having come up from the sea. The beast has seven heads and ten horns. It is described as being like a leopard, with feet like a bear and a mouth like a lion. The beast receives its power from the dragon (the devil).

I believe the beast is the spirit that possesses the Antichrist, but again, I'm not expert on this. I also believe, based on the description of the beast and its origin, that it is an evil angel of the devil. To the point I wish to make, though, I think it's quite easy to agree that the beast—in its original form, at least—is not human.

The second beast, later known as the false prophet, rises out of the earth and receives its power in the same manner as the first beast (from the devil). In Revelation 13:11–12, we find: "And I saw another beast coming up out of the earth and he had two horns, like unto a lamb, and he spake as a dragon And he exerciseth all the authority of the first beast in his sight. And he maketh the earth and them that dwell therein to worship the first beast, whose death-stroke was healed."

I would submit that this second beast, revealed to be the false prophet, is likewise an angel of the devil and not a human being.

So, the three beings that are tormented day and night are the devil and his angels. Scripture clearly states that the eternal fire was prepared for exactly them: the devil and his angels.

The sentence of being tormented day and night is not extended, in Revelation 20:15, to humans. What verse 15 does say is that those whose names were not found in the

Book of Life were cast into the lake of fire. Same thing? No, actually. Not the same at all.

Refer back to verse 14: "And death and hell were cast into the lake of fire. This is the second death."

Verse 14, in its original Koine Greek, is worded ever so slightly differently, but it clarifies the meaning. The verse actually reads, "And death and hades were cast into the lake of fire. This, the second death, is the lake of fire."

The verse defines that the *second death is the lake of fire*. Inversely, the lake of fire is the second death.

The NIV Bible (the best-selling version in the United States) even translates it as such: "Then death and Hades were thrown into the lake of fire. The lake of fire is the second death" (Rev. 20:14).

It's important to understand this definition to understand the eternal punishment that falls upon those whose names are not written in the Book of Life.

Clearly, the devil, the beast, and the false prophet will be tormented day and night forever and ever as their sentence (Rev 20:10).

Those whose names are not found written in the Book of Life will receive a sentence that makes no mention of being tormented. The eternal punishment that they will receive is to be cast into the lake of fire, which is defined as the second death. Read it again: they will be cast into death, not constant torment. The fire that burns eternally for the devil and his angels will bring about the second, and eternal, death for those who are not in the Book of Life (Rev. 20:14–15).

Death, declared by Scripture as the wage of sin, will be paid by those whose names are not in the Book of Life.

Those whose names are in the Book of Life, who had the blood of Jesus cover their sins, thus paying that wage of sin on their behalf, will receive eternal life.

If the lost are to suffer eternally forever, they, too, must possess eternal life. Scripture indicates no such thing for the lost. Rather, scripture says they shall perish. They shall meet a fate just the opposite of eternal life, which is eternal death.

Before we continue to the next parable—lest there be a hang-up on the phrase "eternal punishment," presumed, by way of dogma rather than what Scripture actually says, to mean "eternal torment in the fire of hell," let's address that.

Matthew 25:46 states, "Then they will go away to eternal punishment but the righteous to eternal life."

The "they" in this verse refers to the goats, those whose names are not found in the Book of Life. They will receive eternal punishment.

I'm going to say it again, scripture clearly states that the punishment for sin is death (Rom 6:23). Therefore, what the unsaved will receive is eternal death. Yes, I'm going to continue reiterating that point because reading it the other way (that punishment would be an eternity of burning in hell) is exactly what I did for over five decades, even though that's not what Scripture says. My hope is that you will also break free of that dogma and start accepting what is actually written and not what is assumed.

The term "eternal" is used twice in the verses we just covered, but it is used in two different ways:

1. The eternal fire is the punishment prepared for the devil and his angels.
2. The eternal punishment, for the unrighteous, is the second death.

Eternal punishment, contrary to dogma, does not mean that the *act of punishing* will continue on an ongoing basis for all of eternity, but rather that the *result of the punishment* (death) will be eternal.

The result, not the process, is what is eternal.

Using Scripture to clarify Scripture, in Hebrews 6:2, we find mention of Eternal Judgment. This is referring to the Final Judgment, which will determine whether a person falls among the sheep or the goats for all eternity. The judging portion of Eternal Judgment itself is not repeated on a continual basis with a never-ending trial at the Great White Throne. The Eternal Judgment is executed once, and its results, not its process, are what will be eternal—either eternal life or eternal death.

Hebrews 6:9 speaks of Jesus becoming the author of Eternal Salvation unto all those who obey him. That doesn't mean that a person must go through the process of being repeatedly saved throughout eternity, but rather that the salvation, once received, is for all eternity. Again, *eternal* refers to the result, not the process.

As one final example, 2 Thessalonians 1:8–9 states that at the coming of the Lord, those who have not obeyed the gospel will be punished with Everlasting Destruction. They will not be destroyed, revived, and destroyed again and again every day for eternity. The destruction (complete annihilation) will take place once, and the result, not the process, will be everlasting.

So, it is with Eternal Punishment (which is very much the eternal destruction just mentioned in 2 Thessalonians). It is not the act of punishing (burning in torment forever) that is ongoing for eternity, but rather the result of the punishment (death) that is eternal.

Cast into the lake of fire (the second death), the unrighteous will die, cease to exist. That is the understanding that the disciples would have taken from this parable.

For our next parables, we must first address "weeping and gnashing of teeth," as this phrase is used repeatedly throughout and is taught by church dogma to indicate a state of eternal suffering.

It is very easy to interpret this common phrase from the Bible as meaning that those doing so are experiencing great physical pain and suffering. That, though, is not the context in which the phrase is typically used in Scripture.

Even if it were how it was used, nothing in Scripture indicates that the weeping and gnashing of teeth would be ongoing for eternity. I certainly do not presume that there will not be great emotion when the wicked are cast into the lake of fire, where they will receive their eternal punishment, the second death.

*Weeping*, throughout the Bible, indicates just what it appears to mean: great sadness. *Gnashing of teeth*, though, is used throughout the Bible not as an indication of pain, but rather to express great anger.

In Lamentations 2:16, the enemies of Israel hiss and gnash their teeth, not in pain but in a victorious rage, against Israel after God allowed Israel to be overthrown due to their sin and allowed their enemies to gloat over them.

In Psalms 35:16, the Psalmist, who has suffered greatly, prays that the Lord will deliver him from his enemies, who have gnashed their teeth against him.

In Acts 7:54, as Stephen is about to be stoned to death as a martyr for his faith, he admonishes the Pharisees for their hypocrisy. In response, his accusers are made furious, and they gnash their teeth against him.

There are additional verses that also indicate great wrath and anger as the cause of the gnashing of the teeth.

While I have never attended the sentencing phase of a trial for a serious offense, I have seen many on television. When a verdict or sentence is read, it is often an emotional scene. Weeping and wailing in the courtroom, as well as expressions or acts of anger, come about as the result of the sentence being levied against the guilty.

So, it will be on the Day of Judgment. When the unrighteous hear their sentences, realizing that they are bound for the eternal punishment of death, that they have missed out on the joy of eternal life, there will be emotional responses. As they are cast into the lake of fire (their second, and eternal, death), there will be sadness and regret (weeping) as well as great anger (gnashing of teeth).

While it may sound far-fetched to believe that even at the moment of destruction, sinners would be angry with God rather than pleading for mercy, we find in Revelation 16:9 that those suffering the horrific plagues during the tribulation "cursed the name of God, who had control over these plagues, but they refused to repent and glorify him."

So, it will be on Judgment Day. Even facing destruction, there will be sinners who are unrepentant and who will, in great anger, curse (gnash their teeth) at God.

With that phrasing in context, then, let's move along to the Parable of the Tares (Matt. 13:36–42):

> 36 Then Jesus sent the multitude away and went into the house; and his disciples came unto him, saying, Declare unto us the parable of the tares of the field.
>
> 37 He answered and said unto them, He that soweth the good seed is the Son of Man;
>
> 38 The field is the world; the good seed are the children of the kingdom; but the tares are the children of the wicked one;
>
> 39 The enemy that soweth them is the devil; the harvest is the end of the world; and the reapers are the angels.
>
> 40 As therefore the tares are gathered and burned in the fire; so shall it be in the end of this world.
>
> 41 The Son of Man shall send forth his angels, and they shall gather out of his kingdom all things that offend, and them which do iniquity;
>
> 42 And shall cast them into the furnace of fire: there shall be weeping and gnashing of teeth.

Note that Matthew 13:24–30, the Parable of the Weeds, is a parable so similar that its explanation is the same as is offered here.

The tares (weeds) were planted by the enemy, in the garden of good seed, which was sown by the Son of Man. At the harvest, which is the end of the world, the tares are gathered and burned in the fire, amid cries of sadness and anger.

While this parable does indicate that the weeds (the unrighteous) will be cast into the fire, a common element in Jesus's teachings, nothing therein indicates that eternal conscious torment will take place as a result.

For decades, I read those verses to mean an eternity of suffering would follow being thrown into the fire, just as you may be reading them now. That, though, is not at all what Scripture states, or even to what it alludes. Only if you are basing your interpretation on a preconceived notion of hell, rather what the Scripture actually says, can you arrive at such a conclusion.

As we just read in Revelation 20:14–15, the fire into which they will be cast is the second death.

The weeds (the unrighteous) thrown into the fire would have been understood to burn, not forever, but until fully consumed. The complete destruction of the weeds (the unrighteous) in the fire is exactly how the disciples would have understood and interpreted the parable.

I'm going to say it yet again: there was no concept of a place of eternal suffering in the Jewish religion nor, therefore, in the teachings of Jesus.

It is church dogma rather than biblical teaching that leads to the conclusion that weeds, and therefore the lost, would somehow be preserved to burn forever as punishment.

It's not only church dogma that teaches such a thing, though. Pagan mythology, from the time of the early church and upon which Christian dogma is based (which we will discuss later), also teaches eternal suffering as a penalty of an unrighteous life.

It goes without saying, but pagan mythology is not what Christian beliefs should be based upon.

Be careful to ensure that the Bible, and what it actually says, is your true authority and that your real-life authority is not your doctrine, with the Bible only being read and manipulated in such a way as to support what you already believe.

We read in Matthew 18:8–9:

> 8 Wherefore if thy hand or thy foot offend thee, cut them off, and cast them from thee; it is better for thee to enter into life halt or maimed, rather than having two hands or two feed to be cast into everlasting fire.
>
> 9 And if thine eye offend thee, pluck it out, and cast it from thee; it is better for thee to enter into life with one eye, rather than having two eyes to be cast into hell fire.

In this passage, Jesus declares that if anything causes you to stumble, it is better to cut it off completely, as nothing is worth causing one to miss out on eternal life.

The actual comparison is that it is better to receive eternal life maimed than to be cast into eternal death whole.

We have addressed the everlasting fire of verse 8. In Revelation 20:14–15, those whose names are not in the Book of Life will be cast into the everlasting fire, the second death, where they will miss out on the gift of eternal life.

The hellfire mentioned in verse 9 was actually declared by Jesus as being cast into the fire of Gehenna, in the original Koine Greek text. The KJV translators (surprise!) changed the word to "hell."

The meaning of this verse is that it is better to enter into eternal life, having lost out on something during one's earthly existence, than to be cast into Gehenna, symbolic for the lake of fire, where the carcasses (not the suffering bodies, miraculously preserved alive for the purpose of torment) of God's enemies will be a source of contempt to the righteous. Again, Gehenna was a place of disgraceful death, not a place of continual torment, and "Gehenna" is the word actually spoken by Jesus in the parable.

The disciples, to whom Jesus was teaching the parable, would have understood the symbolic meaning of Gehenna and would have interpreted the outcome of being cast there to mean that those whose fate was Gehenna would be destroyed. In no manner would they have imagined the fate to be an eternal conscious torment. Such an ending had no place in their Jewish-based belief system.

Mark 9:43–48 relays virtually the same message as the previous parable, but in this passage, Jesus proclaims Isaiah's prophecy: "Where the worm dieth not and the fire is not quenched." By incorporating this quote, Jesus tied together the prophecy of Isaiah into an eschatological prophecy incorporating Gehenna as being the place where God's enemies will be looked upon with contempt by the righteous (those who receive eternal life), as the *carcasses* (dead bodies) of those cast into Gehenna (translated, again, as hell, in this passage) burn.

The fire, burning for the devil and his angels, will not be quenched, but there is absolutely no indication (despite the near-universal Christian conclusion of eternal suffering, brought on by errant church dogma) that the unrighteous will burn alive forever.

Again, Gehenna—the place Jesus actually stated was the fate of the unrighteous in this passage—was a place of death (the Biblically declared wage of sin) for God's enemies, not a place of continual torment.

We then find the Parable of the Net in Matthew 13:47–50:

> 47 Again, the kingdom of heaven is like unto a net, that was cast into the sea, and gathered of every kind;
>
> 48 Which, when it was full, they drew to shore, and sat down, and gathered the good into vessels but cast the bad away.
>
> 49 So shall it be at the end of the world: the angels shall come forth, and sever the wicked from among the just,
>
> 50 And shall cast them into the furnace of fire; there shall be weeping and gnashing of teeth.

The good fish are separated into vessels, and the bad fish are cast into the fire.

Just as in the previous parable, the righteous will be separated from the wicked. The former will receive eternal life, and the latter will be cast into the fire (the second death) at the end of the world.

Nothing in the telling of this parable nor in the minds of the disciples to whom Jesus taught it would have suggested the imagery of the fish in the fire being preserved alive to suffer for all eternity. That conclusion is mentally added to the verse by those adhering to the Christian dogma of hell. If we accept Scripture as it is written rather than adding our own ending to it, there is no indication of eternal suffering to be found in this, nor any of the other, Scripture.

In the disciples' interpretation, the fish cast into the fire would have been destroyed. Likewise, the destruction of the wicked at the end of the world is the meaning of this parable.

In Matthew 7:19, Jesus states that "every tree that does not bear good fruit is cut down and thrown into the fire."

We are not in disagreement that being cast into the fire will be the fate of the unfruitful. Where we differ is in what the result of being thrown into the flames will be.

Reading this passage, the obvious conclusion to the fate of the tree is that it will be incinerated into utter destruction, not that it will burn forever and not be consumed.

Taking Scripture as it is written, rather than how you have been conditioned to read it, leads to no imagery of eternal suffering. Such an assumption comes from errant dogma, not from the Word of God.

Please note that in every parable we have covered, there has been no indication that suffering for eternity will be the outcome of those cast into the flames. Unlike in Revelation, where it is plainly stated that the devil and his angels will be tormented day and night forever, there is no such outcome foretold in any of these passages for lost humankind.

If eternal suffering as the fate of the wicked had been included in even one or two of the parables, I'd admit that we could logically place that outcome into the rest of the teachings, as well. That fate, though, is found in absolutely none of the parables! It is the fate of death, destruction, perishing, words which indicate the total annihilation of the wicked, which every parable teaches is the final outcome for the lost.

Church dogma teaches us to take that fate of the devil and apply it to ourselves, but absolutely nowhere does Scripture make that link.

Again, as Jesus taught these parables, he had no word to indicate a place of eternal suffering because no such place existed in the Hebrew Bible upon which Jesus based his teachings. The closest term he had to illustrate the fate of the wicked on the Day of Judgment was Gehenna, and that place was where God's enemies were destroyed. At no point did Jesus expand the imagery of Gehenna to include an eternal suffering by those cast there. He left the message of Gehenna to speak for itself to the disciples, a place of contemptible death and absolute destruction.

Thus, the parables, as they are written and spoken by Jesus, indicate annihilation of the wicked.

It is Christian dogma, not Scripture, that teaches eternal suffering.

There are two additional verses that I wish to address before we move on.

> John 5:28 Marvel not at this; for the hour is coming, in the which all that are in the graves shall hear his voice
> 29 And shall come forth; they that have done good, unto the resurrection of life; and they that have done evil, unto the resurrection of damnation.

While these verses are not a parable of Jesus's, it's important not to leave this loose thread unaddressed because "damnation," a word that is associated almost wholly with Christianity, is defined as "to be cast into hell for an eternity."

It surprised me not at all that the KJV translators used the word *damnation*, as they wished to convey images of hell, but that is not the word used in the original Koine Greek.

The word "damnation," in fact, did not even exist until the 1300s, coming about during the Middle Ages. The church, during that time, created the word and used the threat of eternal damnation to manipulate the population that, again, held a deep fear of (and were controlled by) the imminent, fiery hell that the church so fervently taught.

What was actually written in Koine Greek in the original Scripture was a word that meant "judgment" or "condemnation." The NIV Bible actually translates it as such: "Those who have done what is evil will rise to be condemned."

*Condemned* does not mean eternal suffering. *Condemned* means to be found guilty and sentenced to punishment. As mentioned, numerous times (but, hey, I'm going to say it again), the punishment of sin is death (Rom. 6:23).

What John 5:29 is actually teaching is that at the Resurrection, those who have done good will receive eternal life, and those who have done evil will be condemned to eternal death.

I believe I have covered all the parables in which Jesus taught about hell (er, Gehenna, actually).

In each of them, the fate indicated, if one reads the Scripture as it is actually written, is the destruction of the wicked.

It is only when the mind adds in what is not actually found there, "suffering forever in the flames," that eternal conscious torment comes into play. That addition, though, is based on long-held teaching; it is not based on Scripture.

I'm sure we agree that nothing should be taken away from Scripture to form a doctrine. I would submit that, likewise, nothing should be added to Scripture to form a dogma.

If we allow Scripture to speak for itself, we find no mention of lost humanity burning forever.

If you find a parable to be an exception to the ones I have mentioned here, or if you wish to discuss any opposing thought, or even if you just wish to give me a piece of your mind for daring to challenge church dogma, my email address is provided at the end of this booklet, and I would welcome the opportunity to address any concerns.

I do realize that I have been (and will continue to be) repetitious to a fault. Here I go being repetitive again, but I believe it is going to take hearing, again and again, this opposing view to make any headway against the roughly two thousand years of errant church dogma, courtesy of pagan teachings (more on this later) that have been taught through the ages.

Jesus, our ultimate authority, taught in the parables (if they are accepted as written rather than as imagined) that it will be annihilation, destruction, and death, not eternal suffering, that the wicked will face.

# THE RICH MAN AND LAZARUS

In my attempt to persuade you that eternal suffering in hell is not scriptural teaching, the parable of the Rich Man and Lazarus must certainly be discussed.

This account, found in the Book of Luke, surely demonstrates eternal suffering in hell, doesn't it? Nope, not at all. Let's review (Luke 16:19–31):

> 19 There was a certain rich man, which was clothed in purple and fine linen, and fared sumptuously every day.
>
> 20 And there was a certain beggar named Lazarus, which was laid at his gate full of sores.

21 And desiring to be fed with the crumbs which fell from the rich man's table; moreover the dogs came and licked his sores.

22 And it came to pass, that the beggar died, and was carried by the angels into Abraham's bosom; the rich man also died and was buried.

23 And in hell he lift up his eyes, being in torments, and seeth Abraham afar off, and Lazarus in his bosom.

24 And he cried and said, Father Abraham, have mercy on me, and send Lazarus, that he may dip the tip of his finger in water, and cool my tongue; for I am tormented in this flame.

25 But Abraham said, Son, remember that thou in thy lifetime receivedst thy good things, and likewise Lazarus, evil things; but now he is comforted, and thou art tormented.

26 And beside all this, between us and you there is a great gulf fixed; so that they which would pass from hence to you cannot; neither can they pass to us, that would come from thence.

27 Then he said, I pray thee therefore father, that thou wouldest send him to my father's house:

28 For I have five brethren, that he may testify unto them, lest they also come unto this place of torment.

29 Abraham saith unto him, they have Moses and the prophets; let them hear them.

30 And he said, Nay, father Abraham; but if one went unto them from the dead, they will repent.

31 And he said unto him, If they hear not Moses and the prophets, neither will they be persuaded, though one rose from the dead.

I can almost hear it from you: "Aha! It says it right here *in Scripture* that humankind will be tormented in the flames!"

Yes, it does, but if we take the context and time of the parable into account, we find that this parable has absolutely nothing to do with eternity.

Let's examine a few facts from this parable as well as the origin of it.

In verse 23, the actual word used by Luke was "Hades": "In Hades he lift up his eyes, being in torment..."

Surely, you won't be surprised to learn that the KJV translators changed *Hades* to *hell*.

It is notable, too, that this parable appears only in the Gospel of Luke, not in any of the other synoptic gospels. That is not discrediting in and of itself, but it is worth considering, particularly since, evidently, Jesus used the term *Hades*, very much a pagan Greek concept, rather than using the term *Gehenna*.

We can't ignore that Luke is the only Gentile author of the New Testament.

Luke was born a Greek, raised a Greek, with all the Greek customs and beliefs, and educated as a Greek. And in his Christian ministry, he traveled not to the Jews but, along with Paul, to the Gentiles.

Luke wrote his gospel around AD 90, approximately sixty years after the death of Jesus.

Luke never met Jesus and relied on research and oral traditions to give his account of Jesus's teachings.

As a Greek, Luke would not have been intimately familiar with Gehenna. When it came time for Luke to present someone suffering in the afterlife, he used the Greek term "Hades."

Hades, a concept with which Luke would have been very familiar, was both the Greek god of the underworld and the domain of the afterlife over which he presided.

Hades, the realm, was divided into different areas, and the particular area assigned, whether one of torment or one of bliss, was determined by the deeds of the deceased while they were alive.

The Greeks, unlike the Jews, believed in the immortality of the soul and taught that eternal suffering or eternal bliss were possible outcomes for the dead.

While it seems unlikely that Jesus would abandon Jewish teachings in favor of a mythological Greek realm, as told by Luke, the sole Greek Biblical author, I committed at the outset that I would base my case on what Scripture actually says.

So, I will remain true to that commitment and assume that Luke got every word just right and that Jesus gave an account in which the Rich Man, himself a Jew, was punished according to Greek teachings rather than Jewish ones.

Applying the presumption of full authenticity to this parable, let's examine what it says.

We must begin, again, by noting that *the account does not take place in the realm of eternity*, but rather in the period of time between death and the Final Judgment.

In this passage, we find that Lazarus is not in heaven but instead in Abraham's bosom, a common description of the waiting place between death and Heaven.

Also, the Rich Man asked that Lazarus be allowed to go to his brothers, who were still alive on earth at his father's house, to warn them of the torment that awaited them if they did not change their ways.

Clearly, then, this account takes place prior to the Great White Throne Judgment, and the Rich Man was being punished in an interim place, a purgatory of sorts (although I hold to no belief in the concept of purgatory).

This being the case, this parable has no bearing whatsoever on the concept of eternal suffering in *everlasting* hellfire.

Revelation 20:13, which *does* take place at the Final Judgment, declares, "And the sea gave up the dead which were in it; and death and hell delivered up the dead which were in them; and they were judged every man according to their works."

"Hell" in this verse was actually written as "Hades" in the original Koine Greek before the KJV translators, not surprisingly, transposed it.

So, in this parable, the Rich Man, who Luke declared was in Hades, will be given up on the Day of Judgment, according to Scripture in Revelation 20:13, along with all the other dead that the sea and Hades holds, and they will be judged according to their works.

If it is found that the Rich Man's name is not in the Book of Life, he will be cast into the second death, the lake of fire, where he will be consumed by death, thus paying the wage for his sins.

This parable, quite unlike any other, gives a description of temporary suffering after death while awaiting the Final Judgment.

Perhaps, in his research, Luke came upon the belief among some Jewish rabbis concerning the aforementioned temporary suffering in Gehenna prior to an eternal sentence, and equated that Jewish teaching to his own concept of Hades.

However Luke arrived at his account, it does not give any indication of an *eternity* of torment.

This parable, again, takes place wholly before Final Judgment. Revelation gives us the account of what takes place after Final Judgment.

If, on the Day of Judgment, the Rich Man is cast into the lake of fire, the Second Death will, no doubt, be welcomed as opposed to the pagan Greek–inspired suffering that Luke's account put the Rich Man in while he awaited Final Judgment.

# A HELL OF AN OMISSION FROM THE APOSTLE PAUL

Other than Jesus, no figure is more responsible for the spread of Christianity than the Apostle Paul.

Paul was a devout Jew, a Pharisee, and a member of the Sanhedrin. In the earliest days of Christianity, Paul had actually overseen the murders of Christians for their faith. He was even present at the stoning of Steven, presumably as one of those gnashing their teeth.

After his vision of seeing and communicating with Jesus, followed by his conversion, Paul became just as devout in his Christianity as he had been in his Judaism.

Paul's calling to evangelism, though, was not so much to his fellow Jews as it was to Gentiles throughout the Mediterranean region of the known world.

Paul took the message of salvation through Jesus Christ to the pagans and heathens.

Many of them accepted his message with great enthusiasm! A great many of them, though, having come from a background of Greek culture and teachings, brought along their very Greek-inspired ideas into the church with them.

It was a constant battle, waged through epistles Paul wrote to the various churches, to keep these new converts to the faith in line and away from their old ways and beliefs.

A belief in an afterlife where there was suffering, or bliss, was ingrained into these former pagans. Rather than Christian Jews influencing them to abandon such beliefs, the opposite often occurred. Many Jewish converts to Christianity, who were already turning their traditional beliefs on their head, began to accept the concept of reward and punishment in the afterlife. The foundation of our modern-day belief of hell, as it is presented in Christianity, was solidified as the pagan belief in the afterlife remained mainstream among the gentile converts to the faith.

Paul, though, whose letters to the various churches are our earliest documentation of Christianity, remained true to the Jewish teachings of the afterlife.

In not one of Paul's missionary journeys or in any of the epistles to the various churches did he ever mention hell (or even Gehenna or Hades) as a place of eternal conscious torment in the afterlife.

Consider that fact for a moment. Paul was teaching Christianity 101 to these new converts to this new religion. He was building the early church from the ground up, teaching all the basics of what it means to be a Christian and what traditions and beliefs the Christian faith entailed. In not one word of those fundamental teachings, though, did Paul mention an afterlife of eternal torment for the unbelievers.

Paul spoke plenty about what would be after the return of Jesus, but he never uttered a word about hell.

I imagine the KJV translators absolutely wringing their hands and lying awake at night, just trying to find a way to slip "hell" into the teachings of Paul, but alas, he gave them absolutely no opportunity to do so.

Paul did, though, regularly preach on the wrath of God at the time of judgment.

The wrath of God is a holy and justified response to human sin and disobedience.

The wrath of God was regularly on display in the Hebrew Bible (Old Testament) to which Paul had dedicated his life.

Whenever God's patience with sin came to an end, his wrath followed.

The Great Flood and the destruction of Sodom and Gomorrah are just two of many examples.

What, then, was the result of God's wrath? Complete destruction, absolute death, and total annihilation of the wicked.

Once the limit of God's forbearance has been reached, the complete and utter wiping out of sin, through the destruction (death) of the sinner, has been demonstrated time and time again in Scripture to be God's nature.

Paul taught that the wrath of God would keep one from eternal life (which is the unquestionable result of eternal death), but he never taught that it would lead one to an eternity of suffering.

Certainly, on the Day of Judgment, God's wrath will be on full display; sin will be utterly destroyed, once and for all, never to be resurrected.

Paul made it very clear that through Jesus, whose death on the cross had paid the wage of sin on our behalf, we could avoid the wrath (destruction) of God.

Paul wrote in Romans 5:8–9: "But God commendeth his love toward us in that, while we were yet sinners, Christ died for us. Much more then, being now justified by his blood, we shall be saved from wrath through him."

This was the message that Paul carried to the Gentiles.

As for the Day of Judgment, Paul writes in 2 Thessalonians 1:7–9:

>7 And to you who are troubled, rest with us, when the Lord Jesus shall be revealed from heaven with his mighty angels
>
>8 In flaming fire taking vengeance on them that know not God, and that obey not the gospel of our lord Jesus Christ:
>
>9 Who shall be punished with everlasting destruction from the presence of the Lord, and from the glory of his power…

Paul clearly teaches that, at the coming of the Lord, God will take vengeance on the unrighteous with flaming fire, and they shall be punished with everlasting destruction.

I'm sure you're weary of hearing it from me by this point, but I'm going to say it again. Destruction does not mean preserved alive, in bodily form with all human senses intact, to suffer the torments of hellfire. Come on, now, you know that's not what destruction means.

If it wasn't such a serious misreading, it would be almost laughable that anyone would translate destruction that way, as completely the opposite of what it actually means.

Paul, in his teachings toward the foundation of the church, establishing the very fundamentals of the faith for these new converts, taught that the punishment for those who obey not the gospel of our lord, Jesus Christ, would be everlasting destruction.

I'm going to say it a little louder for those in the back: their punishment will be "destruction"!

Paul preached not just the death of Jesus but also, with much enthusiasm, the resurrection of Jesus. He had a bit of trouble convincing many of the former pagans of the concept that the literal body and soul would be raised from the dead.

The Greek teaching, made popular by Socrates and his pupil Plato, was that the soul of man was immortal. When the body, often a miserable shell that simply housed the soul, died, the soul was set free. To the Greeks, it was the soul that was the true essence of the body, and not the fleshly body itself.

Socrates's teachings held that the body was of little benefit, and those Greek-inspired converts had little desire for their old bodies to be resurrected. They wanted their souls to be free to roam, commune with other souls, and even inhabit new bodies, which would hopefully be even better than their last.

Traditional Jews held the belief that the soul died when the body died. There was no living apart from the body. The soul was simply the life force of the body, but once the body was no more, neither was the soul.

The debate as to whether or not the soul is immortal yet continues, even within Christianity.

Is the soul of man immortal, as the Greeks taught, or is it temporary, as held by the Jews?

Certainly, immortality would be required in some form, even for the wicked, if they are to exist for all of eternity in hell, wouldn't it?

Whether or not the soul of man is immortal may be something else about which we disagree. I have no desire to open yet a whole other can of worms, but I don't side with the former pagans on the issue. As I asked you to agree earlier, Christian doctrine should not be influenced by pagan ideology.

There simply is no Scripture that I can find that declares the soul of man is inherently immortal.

At creation, Man became a living soul, but after the fall in the Garden of Eden, death (mortality) was introduced into the picture, and the soul, like the body, became subject to death.

After casting Adam and Eve out of the Garden, God put angels in place to guard the Tree of Life, lest the fallen humans eat of it and gain immorality (which they had lost because of sin; Gen. 3:22–24).

The author of Ecclesiastes 3:19–20 even goes so far as to proclaim:

> 19 For that which befalleth the sons of men befalleth beasts; even one thing befalleth them: as the

one dieth, so dieth the other; yeah, they have all one breath; so that a man hath no preeminence above a beast; for all is vanity.

20 All go unto one place; all are of the dust and all turn to dust again.

The author of Ecclesiastes taught that man was no different than the animals. Both will die and return to dust. There is no distinction of immortality of body nor soul. Man, it states, has no preeminence (a more lofty or special, set-apart place) above the animals.

Paul, though, definitely believed that the redeemed would rise up out of the dust and, at that point, put on immortality to inherit eternal life.

The belief in the resurrection excited the Apostle Paul, and he taught of it often, perhaps nowhere with more enthusiasm than in 1 Corinthians 15:51–55:

51 Behold, I shew you a mystery; We shall not all sleep, but we shall all be changed.

52 In a moment, in the twinkling of an eye at the last trump; for the trumpet shall sound, and the dead shall be raised incorruptible, and we shall be changed.

> 53 for this corruptible must put on the incorruptible, and this mortal must put on immortality.
>
> 54 So when this corruptible shall have put on incorruption, and this mortal shall have put on immortality, then shall be brought to pass the saying that is written, Death is swallowed up in victory.
>
> 55 O death, where is they sting O grave where is they victory?

Paul clearly teaches that at the resurrection, the mortal must be made immortal. That immortality is what will defeat death for the redeemed.

Death is the wage of sin for the lost. There is, therefore, no logical reasoning by which the lost will put on immortality, as death (the consequence of their unforgiven sin) will not be defeated for them. To receive immortality by the lost would contradict the Bible in that their body or soul would never pay the wage of sin which is, come on, you can say it. Yep, death.

Paul obviously did not hold to the belief that man was inherently immortal. He taught that immortality was something that would have to be received at the Second Coming of Jesus for his bride.

In further support of that view, Paul says that immortality must be patiently sought after and only indicated that it goes to those who will receive eternal life (Rom. 2:5–8):

5 But after thy hardness and impenitent heart treasurest up unto thyself wrath against the day of wrath and revelation of the righteous judgment of God;

6 Who will render to every man according to his deeds;

7 To them who by patient continuance in well doing seek for glory and honour and immortality, eternal life

8 But unto them that are contentious, and do not obey the truth but obey unrighteousness indignation and wrath.

Paul differentiates, in this passage, those who pursue immortality with those who are hard-hearted and obey unrighteousness. The former will receive eternal life. The latter will receive the treasure they have put away for themselves: indignation and wrath (divine judgment that, by the revealed Nature of God, leads to destruction).

Immortality is given as a gift by God to the redeemed in order for them to partake of Eternal Life in heaven.

If all humankind, the redeemed and the unredeemed, inherently possess or would all receive immortality, why did Paul instruct the church at Rome to patiently do good and to seek immortality?

If you overlook the total absence of Scripture supporting that the lost will have immortality simply because the lost *must* take on immortality, in your assessment, as that would be required so that they may suffer the torments of hell forever, please honestly ask yourself if you are basing your belief on Scripture or simply forcing yourself to believe an unsupported concept to accommodate church dogma. Are you relying on what thus sayeth the Word of God, or are you allowing pagan mythology to guide your Christian principles?

Whether you are persuaded on the immortality of humankind or not, let's not forget that Jesus said in Matthew 10:28, "And fear not them which kill the body, but are not able to kill the soul but rather fear him which is able to destroy both soul and body in hell."

That Scripture rather settles the issue. Those who are sentenced to Gehenna, which is what Jesus actually said in this verse, will be destroyed, both body and soul.

Again, the word is *destroy*, and that word does not mean *preserved alive to be tormented*. *Destroy* means *to be brought to destruction*. It truly is that simple.

So, it would seem that even if one presumes the soul to be inherently immortal, Jesus clearly stated that the body and soul will be destroyed in hell, which negates any idea of the soul being inherently eternal in nature.

Throughout his teachings, we find that Paul, like the other disciples, had no concept of eternal suffering in hell. It was his former pagan converts, such as Luke, who, sadly, introduced this Hades-inspired idea into the early church.

# ALL HELL BREAKS LOOSE
## THE APOCALYPSES OF DANIEL AND REVELATION

The books of Daniel and Revelation can be a bit of a head-scratcher, for sure. The symbology and language used are typical of a writing style of the time known as Apocalypses. In prophetic declarations, using otherworldly examples straight out of visions (nightmares!), the writers would foretell future events that they had foreseen.

The Old Testament book of Daniel was drawn on quite heavily by John, the author of Revelation in the New Testament.

Daniel, in his vision, saw the End of Times and the resurrection of the dead at the return of the Lord. In his book, Daniel made the one and only mention of eternal life found in the Old Testament, which was the only indication in the Hebrew Bible that the dead would ever leave Sheol (the grave) and one day live again.

Daniel's vision could only be fulfilled by Jesus, who conquered death, hell, and the grave and thus set free from the captivity of Sheol the departed from all the ages.

While the last several chapters of Daniel document his wild visions with multiheaded beasts and war between mysterious kings and principalities, there is only one passage that is used to substantiate a belief in an eternal hell, so I will address those two verses here (Dan. 12:1–2).

> 1 And at that time shall Michael stand up, the great prince which standeth for the children of thy people: and there shall be a time of trouble, such as never was since there was a nation even to that same time: and at that time thy people shall be delivered, everyone that shall be found written in the book.
>
> 2 And many of them that sleep in the dust of the earth shall awake, some to everlasting life, and some to shame and everlasting contempt.

Verse 2 recalls Isaiah 66:4, in which the prophet declared that the righteous would go out, after a great destruction of the enemy, and look upon the dead that had transgressed against the Lord, and those who were destroyed would be an abhorring to all flesh.

*Abhorring* and *contempt* have very similar meanings: to regard something with disgust, to despise, to scorn.

Daniel's use and Isaiah's prophecies will be fulfilled at the Final Judgment, when the wicked will be destroyed and will be looked upon by the redeemed with contempt and abhorrence.

By no definition does *contempt* mean, in any capacity, *to suffer for all eternity.*

Revelation, like Daniel, is full of multiheaded beasts and the terrible atrocities and sufferings that will occur during the Tribulation.

Again, I make no claim to hold any insight into End Time prophecies, so I will only be addressing the passages that are used in church dogma to support eternal conscious suffering in hell.

OK, let's get right into the passage that gave me the toughest time with which to come to terms. I had lived my life avoiding even peeking into the oh-so-scary book of Revelation, so when I read the following passage (Rev. 15:9–11), it was my first time coming across it. And, boy, is it a doozy!

> 9 A third angel followed them and said in a loud voice: "If anyone worships the beast and its image and receives its mark on their forehead or on their hand,

10 They, too, will drink the wine of God's fury, which has been poured full strength into the cup of his wrath. They will be tormented with burning sulfur in the presence of the holy angels and of the Lamb.

11 And the smoke of their torment will rise for ever and ever. There will be no rest day or night for those who worship the beast and its image, or for anyone who receives the mark of its name."

I must admit, when I first read these verses, I was stumped. I just did not see how that passage could indicate anything other than an eternity of being tormented in hell.

I truly felt, though, that God had opened my eyes to the concept of hell as a place of destruction for humankind rather than a place of torment. I knew, then, that there had to be an explanation for those verses.

I spent the predawn hours praying about that passage, asking God to show me the meaning.

I eventually felt compelled to leave those verses behind for a moment and to keep reading the book of Revelation. As I did so, the verses ahead answered my prayer and helped me to understand what those verses were actually saying!

You may be skeptical about any explanation of Revelation 14:9–11 steering away from eternal torment. I promise not to use smoke and mirrors to explain, but I do have to ask, if you have come this far with me, that you just stay open-minded to the possibility that these verses, too, may be saying something other than what you have been conditioned to believe they are saying.

While the passage certainly sounds—upon first reading and without any other context—like it is taking place at the Great White Throne Judgment and that those in the verses are cast into hell where they are tormented, that actually is not what is happening at all.

To put the passage in context, we must first establish the "tense" and "time."

For tense, let's look at the verbs.

In these verses, the angel declares that if any man *worships* the beast and his image and *receives* his mark on his forehead or his hand, the same *will drink* of the wine of the wrath of God...and he *will be tormented* (while worshipping the beast) with burning sulfur. And the smoke of their torment ascends up for ever and ever, and they have no rest day or night, who *worship* (the actual Koine Greek says "who are worshipping") the beast and his image.

None of these verbs are past tense. Therefore, none are looking back from the standpoint of Final Judgment. All are being used to tell what *will* take place or is taking place in the vision, *not* what has already occurred. If we were at the Final Judgment, John would have been speaking in the past tense and would have stated that the fate befell those who worshipped (past tense) the beast.

John's vision throughout Revelation was laid out sequentially, with a beginning, a middle and an ending.

To understand these verses, we must consider them in their sequential timeframe. The verses we just examined are in chapter 14.

Chapter 16 will add clarification about the fulfillment of those verses in chapter 14, and finally chapter 20 will give the actual and final fate for all those whose names are not found in the Book of Life.

The time, or setting, of chapter 14, as we will see as we read ahead, is during the Great Tribulation, when the actual worshipping of the beast is taking place. Again, verse 11, in its original, pre-translation wording, states that they "will have no rest day or night those who *are worshipping* the beast."

The "no rest day or night" will take place not in eternity, but while they are actively worshipping the beast (during the Tribulation).

Since that beast and the false prophet are cast into the lake of fire before the millennial reign of Christ (Rev. 19:20), then the vision that John saw of those suffering as they worshiped the beast in Revelation 14 (prior to the beast being cast into the fire) takes place at least one thousand years prior to Final Judgment.

Therefore, the suffering day and night is not occurring in hell at all. The passage, in fact, has absolutely nothing to do with eternity.

To put the verses in chapter 14 in context and see what was actually taking place, let's hop ahead to Revelation chapter 16.

In chapter 16, which takes place during the Tribulation, a loud voice from the temple commands the seven angels to pour out the seven bowls of God's wrath on the earth.

The first angel pours out his bowl, and ugly, festering sores break out on the people who took the mark of the beast and were worshipping its image.

The second and third angels pour out their bowls, and the sea and the rivers and springs of water turn to blood.

The fourth angel pours out his bowl, and the sun sends fire, which scorches those who took the mark of the beast and sears their flesh.

The people who had taken the mark curse the name of God but refuse to repent and glorify God.

The fifth angel pours out his bowl, and the kingdom is plunged into absolute darkness.

Scripture then says that those who took the mark of the beast gnaw their tongues in agony and curse God because of the pain from their sores.

The sixth angel pours out his bowl, and the River Euphrates dries up, and demonic spirits come out of the beast and the false prophet.

The seventh angel pours out his bowl, and out of the temple, a loud voice cries, "It is done!"

Then an earthquake unlike any in history occurs, and hail weighing one hundred pounds falls from the sky.

So, we have in chapter 16 a fulfillment of what was foretold and seen in chapter 14. In chapter 16, God's wrath was poured out in the presence of the holy angels (fulfilling Rev. 14:10).

The sun, which contains sulfur as a major element, rained down burning sulfur that seared those who had taken the mark (also prophesied in Rev. 14:10, tormented with fire in the presence of the angels).

Those who had taken the mark of the beast cried out in agony and gnawed their tongues due to the extreme pain from their festering sores, from their skin having been seared by fire, from their water being turned blood, and from being cast into absolute darkness.

Certainly, in this vision of undergoing the wrath of God being poured out during the Tribulation, those who had taken the mark were having no rest, day or night, as foretold in Rev. 14:11.

Hopefully, you can agree that the verses in chapter 14 (which occured before the beast was cast into the lake of fire and brimstone, more than a thousand years prior to the Final Judgment) are *not* taking place at the Great White Throne Judgment. Therefore chapter 14 is not an account of what is happening in the realm of eternity.

The torment of Chapter 14 is taking place during the Great Tribulation.

Once that understanding is established, those verses can be read in a very different way than if they are taken as a stand-alone passage, completely out of context.

We've already discussed Revelation 20:10 and 20:14–15, but I'm going to include the explanation here again. It, along with the verse we just discussed, is absolutely one of the strongest passages that would lead one to believe the dogma of eternal conscious torment in hell.

Revelation 20:10 is the only place in the entire Bible that mentions being tormented day and night forever. That fate is limited to the devil and his angels, but the image has been mentally added to nearly every passage concerning hell throughout the Bible, as if it applies to all of lost humankind.

That verse, along with the images passed down, generation to generation, from Dante's *Inferno*, constitutes almost our entire concept of hell. Revelation 20:10 states, "And the devil that deceived them was cast into the lake of fire and brimstone, where the beast and the false prophet are, and shall be tormented day and night for ever and ever." And Revelation 20:14–15 states, "And death and hell were cast into the lake of fire. This is the second death. And whosoever was not found written in the book of life was cast into the lake of fire."

Revelation 20:10 states that it is specifically the devil, the beast, and the false prophet who will be tormented day and night forever and ever.

Matthew 25:41 specifically states that the eternal fire was prepared for the devil and his angels. While it's true that the wicked will be cast into that fire, as we are about to discuss, their fate is different than the devil's.

As I've said time and time again, the fate of the wicked is death (the wage of sin) from the fire.

Verse 15 applies to those whose names were not found in the Book of Life. Scripture absolutely does not extend the same fate to the lost as it does to the devil.

What verse 20:15 does say is that those whose names were not found in the Book of Life were cast into the lake of fire, which truly is not the same thing.

Refer back to verse 20:14: "Then death and Hades were thrown in to the lake of fire. The lake of fire is the second death" (NIV).

The Eternal Judgment sentence that awaits the unrighteous, then, is separate from the one that awaits the devil.

The devil, the beast, and the false prophet will be tormented day and night forever and ever in the lake of fire and brimstone as their sentence.

Those whose names were not found in the Book of Life will receive a different sentence. They will be cast into the second death (the scriptural definition of the lake of fire), a place where they will be destroyed (suffer their second death) forever.

The fire that torments the devil day and night forever and ever will bring about the wage of sin for the lost. That wage (yep, I'm really going to say it again) is death (Rom. 6:23).

If you still believe me to be in error, wait until you hear this next thought.

As I've already gone out on a limb, I'm gonna dare to go even farther and say that I'm not at all certain that the torment that the devil and his angels will suffer will be eternal physical pain. I'm just not sure that God puts such a horrific penalty on any of his Creation.

Ezekiel 10:7 talks of angels taking up fire and holding it in their hands without any indication that they suffer pain or are burned. Angels, including the devil, are spiritual beings, and there is no indication that they possess nerve endings such as we have in our human bodies, which would be necessary to suffer physical pain.

2 Peter 2:7–9 speaks of Lot being tormented day and night by the deeds of the wicked in Sodom.

Tormented, in the case of Lot, did not mean he was in great physical pain but, rather, that he was gripped by great emotional sadness for the state in which he found himself.

The torment that the devil and his angels suffer both day and night may very well be deep, perpetual sadness and regret at having forever fallen from the presence of God.

I mention that strictly as an aside and present it as a possibility that the Scripture could be interpreted that way. Unlike my unwavering stance of hell being destruction rather than suffering, I don't hold fast to this latest curveball as positively being the case.

Knowing the love of God, however, it won't surprise me if he sends none, not even the devil, to suffer unending physical pain.

# CONCLUSION

We serve a God of infinite mercy and grace. His love knows no limits.

Nowhere in his Word does he state that humankind will be tormented forever and ever. That fate is reserved, the *one time* it is mentioned in scripture, for the devil and his angels.

It is Christian dogma, brought into the early church by the converted pagans, that teaches such a ghastly thing.

Certainly, through twisted readings, misinterpretations, and long-established assumptions, we can allude to eternal torment, but nowhere, when Scripture is accepted for what it actually says, is that message actually conveyed.

Reading "eternal conscious torment" into the various Scriptures requires that we completely redefine the words *perish*, *death*, and *destruction* to mean the opposites of their actual definitions. To accommodate Christian dogma concerning hell, we must read these words, which indicate total annihilation, as if they actually mean an immortal, eternal life lived in torment. To do so requires willful ignorance.

God never spoke of hell in the Old Testament.

Jesus symbolically taught the annihilation of the wicked in Gehenna in his parables.

Paul warned of God's wrath, which would lead to destruction, but never taught, even one single time, about hell in any capacity.

Those messages, all which completely lack a teaching of hell, are the true foundation of our faith.

After the conquest of Palestine by Alexander the Great around 330 BC, during the Intertestamental Period, Jews began to become influenced by Greek ideas.

With pressure to abandon their faith, many Jews did stray and did adopt the ideology, customs, language, and beliefs of the Greeks. One of the most appealing ideas for the Jews was the Greek teachings of an afterlife in which the righteous would be rewarded and the wicked would be punished.

Jews, throughout their history, had suffered at the hands of ungodly rulers, and the idea that in the afterlife, the evil conquerors would be punished, while God's people would receive great reward, was a concept—even though it had no basis in Scripture—that they were happy to adopt.

By the time of Jesus, there were some Jews who believed, at least in part, in the Greek concept of the afterlife.

Jesus, however, would not have been one of them. His teachings were true to the Hebrew Bible.

The early church, built upon the teachings of Jesus, held no belief of hell as we know it today.

It was only after Christianity grew from a small Jewish sect to a predominantly Gentile religion that the pagan traditions of Hades (hell, as the KJV translators would say) were brought into the church's teachings as fundamental doctrine.

The Catholic Church, which eventually became the official religion of the Roman Empire following the conversion of Emperor Constantine, was up and running as early as AD 55, barely two decades after the death of Jesus.

Made up almost wholly of Gentiles, who were former pagans steeped in Greek mythology, and having very little Jewish influence by this point, Christianity was embracing the idea of eternal conscious torment in hell almost from the start.

When the Protestant Reformation took place in the sixteenth century, the Reformers abandoned a great many of the beliefs of the Catholic Church, from which they split.

The concept of hell as a place of eternal conscious torment, though, was one belief to which they held tightly.

Unfortunately, to this day, the church has never recovered from the introduction of this Greek-inspired false teaching.

# AFTERWORD

First of all, I'd like to thank you for reading until the end. It is not easy to listen to, much less consider, an opposing view of any kind, and particularly a view that goes against long-held theology.

I do hope that my position hasn't angered you.

I also hope that I have caused you to at least consider that perhaps the dogma of hell, as it has been taught for nearly two thousand years, might deserve a second look.

I prayed very much about sharing my thoughts and did so in hopes primarily that anyone who suffers from stygiophobia, the mental torment stemming from the fear of hell (commonly as the result of religious indoctrination), might find some relief.

Certainly, hell deserves sincere consideration. An eternal death, forever away from the everlasting joy of being in God's presence, is no small thing. The destruction that takes place at the second death will, no doubt, be horrific as well.

Still, a mind set free from the fear of an eternity of immense suffering has been one of the most blessed things God has ever given me.

As stated previously, since coming to this realization, I love Him even more deeply and appreciate His mercy all the more.

I believe He has spoken to me more clearly on this subject than anything else for which I have sought Him.

If you'd like to discuss my views, to share your thoughts, or even to admonish me for having such a mindset, feel free to contact me at smpenn1968@gmail.com.

God bless.

www.ingramcontent.com/pod-product-compliance
Lightning Source LLC
LaVergne TN
LVHW020452070526
838199LV00063B/4921